DianaText
.Com

*Published In the United Kingdom
by Diana Text & Co*

First Published 2016

All rights reserved. No part of this publication maybe reproduced, stored in a retrieval system, or transmitted, in any form or by any means. Within the UK, exceptions are allowed in respect of any fair dealing for the purposes of research or private study, or criticism or review, as permitted under the Copyright, Designs and Patens Act, 1988, or in the case of reprographic reproduction in accordance with the terms of the licenses issued by the Copyright Licensing Agency. Inquiries concerning reproduction outside these terms and in other countries should be sent to the Rights Department Diana Text & Co Publications, at the address below.

This book is sold subject to the condition that it shall not, by way of trade or otherwise, be lent, resold, hired out or otherwise circulated without the publisher's prior consent in any form of binding or cover other than in which it is published and without a similar condition including this condition being imposed on the subsequent purchaser

Diana Text & Co Publications
Newark
Nottinghamshire
United Kingdom
2016

Table of contents

Introduction

SUN MOON & TALIA
William Le'shon's Sleeping Beauty
'The Real Sleeping Beauty' (2016)
& Introductory Analysis

SOLE LUNA E TALIA
Benedetto Croce's Sleeping Beauty
Modern Italian Edition (1932)

SOLE LUNA E TALIA
Giovan Battista Basile's Sleeping Beauty
'Lo Cunto De Li Cunti' (1634)

Diana Text & Co Publications
Newark
Nottinghamshire
United Kingdom
2016

Introduction

With there being many copies, editions and re-editions of Giovan Battista Basile's *Sun Moon and Talia* (1634), I thought it would be convenient for writers and people with a general interest in fairy-tales to have access to Basile's original Sleeping Beauty; Benedetto Croce's modern Italian, and, an English translation: all in one place. Moreover, a Sleeping Beauty edition that has had much of its fluffy render stripped away. Maintaining only enough core narrative to retain the essence of a consistent, yet concise story.

The English translation is plain. Purposely. In this way writers may generate their own Sleeping Beauty without having to check or recheck through the various online and physically published editions for validation on a given point. This stripping of the meat also eased the job of cross referencing the keywords and phrases fundamental to the formation of the mythemes found in the Sleeping Beauty text. This was still a slow and laborious process however, the excavation of the major mythemes, should, once again, make life much simpler for a busy creative who wants to just get on with producing their own composition.

As it happens the methodology undertook for this project was fairly straightforward. As it ought to be. With the primary analysis concentrating on Basile's original *Lo Cunto de li Cunti*, it was nevertheless necessary to check for consistencies to much earlier Sleeping Beauty publications; and, also to examine text outside the Sleeping Beauty cycle e.g. Andrea Perrucci's *Treaties on Memory* (1699).

This unavoidable straying has resulted in brining clarity to a text that has seen many transformations. Changes inevitably brought about through its manifold transmissions to an unstatic reception. This is not a corruption of the text, as the Sleeping Beauty cycle is very much alive, yet in order for Sleeping Beauty to maintain its external heart beat, its internal text is required to mould and remould itself to the shifting tastes of its audience. Inescapably keywords become dislodged or omitted, with the consequence of misdirecting the historic meaning which lays just under the text's surface. As an example: there tends to be in the various modern Sleeping Beauty translations some ambiguity and confusion on whether it was Talia's son, or her daughter, who was responsible for waking the Sleeping Beauty through sucking out the spinner's flex. So where Basile uses the word, 'volenno', he means to deploy the phrase, 'when he tries':

> li quale, na vota, **volenno** [when he tries] zucare ne trovanno lo capetiello, l'afferra o lo dito e tanto zu caro che ne tir aro l'aresta

> The fates (fairies) compelled him [volenno] to grab the finger and suck out the silver flex

Why Sun and not Moon woke the sleeping Talia is something of a broad subject in itself and was dealt with in detail in my previous book, *The Real Sleeping Beauty, Her Meaning & History*. Within this same publication I lightly touch upon Charles Perrault's 1697 Sleeping Beauty edition, which as any self interested party of the Sleeping Beauty cycle can attest, was the influence behind Walt Disney's cartoon feature: whereby Talia's son is usurped for a young handsome prince. We shall not go much further into this subject matter, as our introductory analysis is intended only to focus upon Basile's text.

By setting a limitation on extracting esoteric meaning solely from Basile's Sleeping Beauty edition, is no easy task either. That most historical and religious themes, and there really is quite a lot of them, can only be fully appreciated with corpus citations and comparative analysis. However, I see no absolute reason why we should view this difficulty as an unbreakable barrier, although this short introductory overview does not, in anyway, give this Sleeping Beauty edition the full justice it deserves.

Nevertheless. There is a large amount of material in which to sieve through before we can begin to distil the fundamental mythemes. And we start with the same question always arising at these first steps into any given composition: which mythemes should we take as worthy threads, samples for us to begin conducting our investigation? We could argue the fate given over to Sleeping Beauty's father at the text's beginning is a worthy candidate, or maybe all the key features should be equally treated as a mytheme nucleolus, and to a certain extent this is true.

But, if we took every twist and turn as a mytheme, we would muddy the water and, once all the threads were lined up for our bird's eye analysis, we would probably have just created a text summary. The intention is to draw out mythemes onto which the narrative aligns its overall trajectory, the ones who compensate for Sleeping Beauty's twists and turns; in short: the focal points which maintain fusion.

Then if we were to extract these narrative eddies, separating them yet preserving their alignment in the same order they were originally deployed, we should find a clear running river of text we could easily navigate. A course clearly mapped from where we can attain a heightened understanding on what was the primary purpose behind the narrative's meaning at its time of conception.

Let us look first at how Sleeping Beauty is woken by her child, her son. In the story's earlier versions, he may or may not have been assigned the proper noun, Sun. That is because of the obvious agricultural undertones in this section, we as modern readers would reasonably assume Sleeping Beauty's son was given this name purely on this rustic theme. Indeed, every contemporary child is taught that the sun's light is an inextricable component, not just for plant growth, but also as a heat source for a seedling's germination.

But this is modern logical fallacy, a will-o'-the-wisp. For many ancient cultures it was the blue coloured moon held responsible for the water cycle from which all life was thought to generate within, and emanate from. On the contrary, within their daily experience the sun's heat withered and killed a plant through magically removing its internal 'life-water', sap.

Heat was believed to have a detrimental effect on a plant's life cycle, especially in the hot dry Mesopotamian landscapes where widespread farming techniques were first practiced. Certainly, away from the relative coolness of the lush green river valleys and further removed from the irrigated flood plains, the lands surrounding agricultural outposts were parched dry spaces; baked deserts, utterly devoid of plants due to the absence of life giving water.

There were also similar beliefs held by the ancient people who tilled the Nile's banks, and others too within the ancient world, so for these reasons – in my book mentioned above, I propose, with the presented evidence, Sleeping Beauty is an ancient text from a desert region -

Sleeping Beauty's baby boy could easily have been named, Moon. Yet this ambiguity changes little on his meaningful role, a single action which on its own implies that the original story, still embedded within Basile text, must necessarily have been related to an early agricultural myth. The sucking out of the splinter and waking Talia is a metaphor of plant growth after the dormancy of winter; we shall catalogue the waking Talia as mytheme 1 (M#1).

Another mytheme comes prior to Sleeping Beauty being woken, and is the moment at which she is impregnated. These few verses have always been a highly controversial theme. Even during the early Middle Ages when the text of Sleeping Beauty was embedded within the book *Perceforest*. For this introductory publication we shall not be dealing with these verses in any detail, there needs to be extensive contextual ground work covered before they yield their true meaning. Yet what can briefly be stated here is that mythemes of non-consensual sex were deployed quite often during the ancient and medieval periods. They were placed into a text or a myth for various reasons and require analysis on a point by point bases: that there is no one fits all generalisation on the why they were used, nor, why this mytheme could be deployed more blatant than at other times.

This variation in subtlety can sometimes be so vague that the mytheme is deployed without notice and continues to exist in transmission, devoid of any sense of controversy. For example, the impregnation of Jesus' mother, Mary. In the biblical text, Mary is non-consensually fertilised by the Christian god-head; the verses imply her free will, her own free choice, is not even of secondary consideration. More blatantly, a similar fate befell many beautiful maidens who'd caught the insatiable eye of the god-head Zeus, or the high libido Sumerian god-head, Enki, etc.

Nevertheless, we now have two mythemes: the impregnation of Sleeping Beauty (M#2) and her later waking moment though the spinners flex being sucked from her finger (M#1). There will shortly be a further two mythemes elucidated. However, to fully appreciate them, to see them for what they truly are, we would greatly benefit from first analysing the major characters who populate Basile's text.

That if we compartmentalise and contrast them in ways to thoroughly illuminate their character role, their point of purpose for existing within Basile's Sleeping Beauty, then the two final mythemes shall stand out in greater clarity then what they would otherwise. To these ends we are going to assign to each single character a counter character of equal social standing. Couplets attached to their opposite number from which a list of binary opposites can be drawn; thus for example: Cook vs. king's Assistant and Queen vs. Talia, etc.

As a caveat, viewed in isolation, binary opposites are limited only to magnifying character traits such as personal ambition, character flaws - if any - their strengths and weaknesses. However, when they are placed into the wider context of the text's narration, we can often infer possible characteristics that were perhaps to vague to notice, or even omitted from the composition a text had evolved.

Moreover, where these binary opposites are at their most extreme, i.e. bringing to conclusion their antagonism or reinforcing their superlative qualities, there is more often than not the presence of an inflection, i.e. an indication of a mytheme. So, without further ado, let us now look at these binary opposites. Beginning with the Cook vs. king's Assistant. A couplet whose disparity is a major component of the mytheme which will be introduce after their analysis.

To start with, it should go without saying that a king's Assistant would be dependable, trustworthy and beyond reproach; up to and even sacrificing their own life for those cherished patriotisms, or at the very minimum, withdrawing their person from a sovereign's inner circle if they believed their presence could somehow bring unnecessary risk to their king.

Yet, despite these supposed prerequisite qualities, we are informed through explicit detail that the king's Assistant, when faced with physical threats to dislodge his loyalty, immediately bows to the Queen's demands. Then if that wasn't enough, he moves beyond the realms of disloyalty to eagerly embrace the Queen's orders for personal gain: actively engaging with the her devious plans. With little persuasion he switch's sides, becoming not just a traitor, but also transformed into an enabler of injustice.

The traits of the king's Assistant indirectly tell us much about the other characters within Basile's text: whereby the Assistant's appointment lends us insightful information about the young King's inner personality, particularly at the texts' beginning. We can infer the young King as naive and inexperienced, a poor judge of character. Contrast the Assistant to the moment when the King orders the Cook to be thrown onto the fire. The Cook speaks eloquently, with wit and projected strength. This is not the vernacular, grace or stature we would expect from a lowly kitchen worker; and it is not as though the Cook, unlike the young King, has gone through some progressive rite of passage.

The Cook did not undergo an epiphany. He had not been newly reborn as a Cook with elevated personal virtues, the text makes no mention on these things nor can they be inferred. So, when we read the Cook speaking truth to power, and, moreover, his disobedience to the Queen's morbid command, we are witnessing a man who'd always held strong moral beliefs. He is not a fox who calculates personal cost to benefit ratios; he humbly weighs concepts at their most reduced level: are they good, or are they bad?

His simple matrix of absolutes is played out on the Cook's most prominent judgement call, the fate pertaining to the young King's children. The Cook doesn't seem to make any evaluation when risking his own life to the save the lives of Sun and Moon. This implies a selfless act.

Indeed, the text says only he felt pity for Sleeping Beauty's children. Nothing can be inferred as him choosing a riskier path in order to advance his own personal standing. This inference is later reinforced when the young King rewards the Cook, and not only from stopping the act of cannibalism, but also through the young King being impressed by the Cook's wit and stature, standing up for himself in a dignified and proper manner. Thus, as the Assistant told us much about the young King at the text's beginning, the Cook informs us much on the transformation experienced by the young King at the narratives' end. That by recognising the Cook's up standing attributes, and rewarding them through an elevation of the Cooks social station and personal wealth, then the young King is showing himself to have become a good judge of character.

A metamorphosis born out in a limited way from the antagonisms which exist between Cook and Assistant, a strife that reaches its climatic moment during the young Kings feast; the inflection point of cannibalistic infanticide. This indirect conflict between the competing servants could be argued as them being mere foils, literary devices whose sole purpose is to add depth and contrast to the other major characters, however, the Cook's role is far more profound than a simple man made good through correctly navigating with a moral compass.

To reference Lévi-Strauss. He worked on cooking themes embedded both in the documented forms and the vibrant living myths of oral tradition;

mostly sourced from hunter gathering tribes of South America. From his research, Strauss concluded that cooked food is best described as culture, while raw food, its antithetical binary opposite: wild nature. Building upon this basic premise he developed a framework whereby tribal cooks are more than mere kitchen servants; they are social enablers. People who in mythical contexts take an object from the chaotic untamed world of nature, then through a process of socialisation, produce the stuff of culture.

If we apply this Straussian model onto the Cook from Sleeping Beauty, he then represents a person of high intellect, a philosopher, a hierophant, a man of many talents. An archetypal mythical cook whose character traits are marked through his virtuous choices, his rewards and in the way he chooses his cooking methods when substituting Sun and Moon for kid goats: he socially transforms them not just once, but in a 'hundred different ways'.

Even the decision to cook young goats also informs us much about the religious connotations surrounding Sleeping Beauty's

Cook, in that historically, influential cultures near and around the Mediterranean basin preferred using lamb as their sacrificial animal of choice. This preference for young beasts came down from the animal's propensity for retaining their tenderness during and after the roasting process. While meat from older animals tends to be tough and near inedible. Consequently, older chewy meat had been viewed as an unworthy offering to their respective deities.

Indeed, as far as the Mesopotamians were concerned, this ritual quality control developed into a form of invoicing used to pay debts incurred from goods and services procured by the State apparatus for its day to day administrative needs. Succulent sacrificed lamb went to the aristocrats, while mutton and old goat were consumed by the lower classes. There was though, no dogmatic objection for utilising goat kids as sacrificial offerings. Their infrequent use stems from them being economically active throughout their adult life, being the producers of valuable dairy products such as milk and cheese; products which were themselves seen as delicacies ideally adopted for votive offerings.

Typically, goats would not be sacrificed, or secularly slaughtered until late into their adult life when their meat was rendered un-conducive for ritual practices. However, although luscious goat kids were on august occasions ritually sacrificed, their soft juicy meat would only be served to high ranking officials and/or Mesopotamian kings. With these references kept in mind, our Cook's choice of animal is probably a deliberate innuendo to this cultural practice, as bread and water has become synonymous of ascetic imagery.

In *The Real Sleeping Beauty, Her Meaning & History*, I delve deeper into the cultural and anthropological significances of animal and human sacrifice, drawing upon how these universal institutions are the roots from which grow many of our inherited religious rites and mythical narratives, of which, the cannibalism mytheme in Basile's Sleeping Beauty, is a prime example; and we'll classify this cannibalism as a mytheme (M#3).

Returning now to the binary opposites. The character couplet which exists between the

Queen and Talia is perhaps the most conspicuous. While at first sight this overtness may look to be skewed toward the bellicose forces emanating from the Queen, it is because of this imbalance we are surreptitiously informed about Talia's passive character. In an almost subliminal manner we see the princess's superlative qualities. A personality who seems to be constantly swept along by deterministic events. She is rendered hopelessly weak, and, unfortunate.

While our Queen on the other hand is portrayed as all powerful, domineering and seemingly in full control of her destiny. She has total free will. On one level Talia's fatalism bolsters the corollary of the brutishly cruel Queen: cunning and envious. While on a deeper level the subtext implies the Queen to be either barren or unable to sexually arouse her husband - they have a childless marriage.

We can take for granted the Queen is from a noble family, however, and much to the young King's annoyance, she has brought to their marriage little or no personal wealth. Why then did the young King marry her? Indeed, this is not a rhetorical question, it is brought to the forefront in the Sleeping Beauty text; yet just left hanging without being expressly answered.

But on further analysis, this unsettled question does lend itself to juxtapose, or if you will, broaden the contrasting features between the Queen and her antagonist; that her cruelty, cunning and greed, compounds her parasitical non-mutual relationship with her husband, the young King.

The Queen is a source of imbalance, harbinger of chaos, a barren empty shell, a life consumer. While Talia is fertile, youthful, beautiful, compassionate, forgiving, bringer of balance and of course, she is endowed with the airs of innocence.

So with that said, is there anything we can say directly about Talia without further reading and spoiling what is in the book mentioned above? Let us answer this question with another question: did Talia defy her father's wishes by handling the old lady's distaff? Because it would seem strange for the old, *'wise King'*, to have had prior knowledge on some ill fate stemming from a weaver's spindle. That after going through so much trouble and effort to banish these textile objects from his near kingdom and palace grounds, that this *'wise'* old King fails to do one simple task, a thing so obvious: inform Talia on the dangers posed from her handling a distaff.

Another curious feature which equally deserves additional attention is when the Queen orders Talia to be thrown into the roaring flames. Talia interjects, she requests a short stay of execution so that she may remove her embroidered dress. Is Talia so innocent, so unaware of worldly matters she believes she shall be able to put her clothes back on after she'd been thrown onto the fire? Or maybe Talia is so materialistic she worries more for her worldly processions than her own life? Neither of these two solutions feel adequate.

Tellingly Talia chants - written as woes - when she removes an item of clothing. Perhaps then she has some knowledge of the dark arts? However, what I believe we can safely say about Talia, she had adequately evaluated the Queen.

Surmising her to be shallow and materialistic and so manipulates her, taking some control on the events as they unfold, buying herself enough spare time for her to be saved, and then, as we further read, a complete reversal on the executioner and condemned scenario. This twisting of the plot at this exact moment is our final mytheme (M#4).

Talia is no doubt a good judge of character. We can infer then, Talia is not so innocent as we were led to believe. This could be as a result of her knowing something of the fates which await her and embraces them with vehement passion. Does she secretly hold an advantage, manipulating circumstance for her own ends? These are very valid questions which shall not be fully answered in this introductory publication. But, as we now begin to build-up the alignment of mythemes M#1-M#4, we'll get a glimpse of Taila's true nature.

Still. Who do we suppose is the binary opposite relating to the young King? Recalling Assistant vs Cook, Queen vs Talia have already been assigned. What character is now left for us to contrast, albeit in a balanced manner, the attributes pertaining to our young King? Again, I am going to answer this question with yet another question: what purpose do stories serve? This is a perennial question that may have as many answers as the amount of years it has been repeatedly asked, but with that said, most bibliophiles would agree on some basic tenets.

For example, sometimes a story can be for pure entertainment or used as practical script; but often, especially in regards to ancient narrations, they are encyclopaedic vessels into which a people store their entire knowledge base, pertaining to, but not necessarily limited for, religious and ethical answers to the temporal reality they find themselves occupying. Drawing elicit existential meaning, justifications for this that, and the other.

From this type of corpus, a social group will use them as tools to convey solutions to an everyday problem, in much the same way a modern engineer or astronaut will use a flow chart. Let me expand and broaden out this trail of thought by taking the Homeric hymn to Demeter as a working example. On a superficial level this is a story about a mother's devotion to her daughter, but on a more profound level, the story is a means for explaining why crops lay dormant during the winter, break the soil in spring so they may ripen and be harvested during the summer. A primordial version of an agricultural text book.

What has occurred, and particularly quickened in the past 100 years, is that the Homeric hymn has been broadened and fragmented as specialised subjects such as botany, biology, genetics, chemistry and soil physics, etc.

At times, we could find a story embedded with a pick and mix of those limited examples mentioned above, yet what unites each and every purpose of a narrative is its intrinsic need for a recipient, a reader, or more specifically, a receptive audience on which an impressionable narrative can express its meaning, the young King's binary opposite, is us, the audience.

Accepting we are the young King's binary opposite, then logically should not the young King's attributes in some way be the polar-opposite of how we see ourselves? And indeed, we do. An experience which reaches its zenith when the young King's hubris enables him to copulate with the sleeping Talia, an act so repulsing, and so appalling, Basile took to writing these verses as a hazy vague passage:

> All along the young King kept admiring her beauty. Soon he turned to lust. Picking her up, he carried the sleeping Talia to her bed, then took the fruits of love.

[Sun Moon and Talia §7]

Evidently, Basile did not wish to generate too much alienation through exposing his audience to the full extent on how far removed the young King had gone from the centre of contemporary virtue. So Basile struck a balance by installing vagueness. No doubt he was aware that without this verse, his Sleeping Beauty edition would have lost much of its essential meaning and its historical pedigree. As evidenced by the Walt Disney's rendering, which is almost impossible to decipher when viewed with no references to the previous Sleeping Beauty editions.

Even so, Basile's hazy copulation still works. He retains a couplet between the young King and the audience, one based, not on absolute antagonisms, but a system drawn from dynamic emotion: there is a recoil followed by a reconciliation; so that as our young King shifts from selfish fiend to hero King, we too are shifted along with him: from repulsion to apathy, and finally, we experience sympathy. There is an intended resonance connecting the audience to the text.

This is a clever literary technique, bearing in mind the audience is not being forcefully bent to suit the narrator's ends. They must be a willing participant, otherwise we would simply reject the future hero King out of hand, and instead, experience, as we do with the Queen, an absolute antagonism.

I am now at a point where I am hesitant to go any further on the analysis of this particular mytheme, that more information needs to be drawn from the other versions of Sleeping Beauty before this section's meaning begins to make sense, and even then, this will only be an imprecise picture. It is only when all the accompanied texts are interpreted in light of anthropological data from outside the Sleeping Beauty cycle, will a fully complete understanding be reached; so, for now we shall swiftly move-on to the next binary opposite, the fruits from this copulation: Talia's twins.

This binary opposite, Sun vs. Moon, is so straightforward we should pause with caution, raising an eyebrow, or two, as we proceed with our analysis. The children are male and female, not an unusual association in the sense of celestial twins in myth and folklore in general; however, I fear we could be led into over analysing their binary opposite roles, believing them, from a theoretical framework, to somehow represent universal dualistic concepts or some and such.

Because by a quick examination on their comparative roles, when listed as literary objects, Sun and Moon are mere bystanders. They literally say nothing and act only in a few scenes; and even then only one character was necessary. Yet in terms of historic symbolism, their role is crucial to the overall plot and their absence on the effect of other characters would render many features found within the narration as meaningless topics.

The son wakes Talia, while the combined entities, Sun and Moon, instigate the cannibalism conspiracy, which simultaneously exposes the positive contributions made by the Cook and the negative aspects rooted from both the Assistant, and the Queen. We see this topic change emphasis in other versions of Sleeping Beauty. Where the Sun and Moon's presence is drastically different; in *Perceforest* there are no twins, just a boy, while for Perrault's version the twins are not Talia's children but simple passers-by who happened to enter Talia's sleeping chamber to fulfil a childish curiosity.

Perrault probably applied this narrative direction because it would allow him to omit the copulation scene which he may have thought too morally outrageous for his intended audience. While for the Mesopotamian version, *Inanna & Sukaletuda*, there are no physical children to speak; yet this most ancient edition does give birth to a child, albeit abstract in form and character, balanced and in tune with natural phenomena - ontologically speaking.

The children of Basile's Sleeping Beauty is implying some sort of celestial intervention, a fate decreed that is being epitomised with his use of the proper nouns: Sun and Moon. Obviously the story has an inherent agricultural dimension pertaining to the son, named after one or other of these celestial bodies. The boy sucking out the flex from Talia's finger is a metaphor to invoke in the audience's mind, spring growth. This is an important feature from the original narrative collected by Basile which I believe he wished to retain. While at the same time, he stripped away other features he thought to overtly pagan. The cumulative consequence of his rewriting and balancing acts was to generate a semi esoteric genre we now call: 'fairly-tale'.

However, for us to fully appreciate *Sun Moon and Talia* in general and Sleeping Beauty in particular, we need to start investigating these astrological links in a little more detail. But before we delve deeper into the celestial analysis, I want us first to summarise our binary opposites so that we do not lose track on what additional information we have extruded thus far:

Sun and Moon are not absolute binary opposites, they are more chiral in nature, complementary mirror images who are in a fixed state. We would designate them as: *in-balance.*

The young King and Audience are also not complete binary opposites, but form a more dynamic reflection whereby their interaction ebbs and flows, eventually they gravitate toward one another, giving a resultant emotion that brings the senses: *in-balance.*

Cook and Assistant are more indirect antagonists. This dynamic comes to the fro when we read further into their relevant passages, a contrast which grows with each passing word; we could then, with literary validation, call them incremental antagonists. Negative dynamic poles, true binary opposites who are always: *out-of-balance.*

Talia and Queen are absolute antagonists. A couplet whose relationship resembles strongly the Cook and Assistant paradigm just mentioned, but with their negative interplay being overtly obvious, that as we move through the Sleeping Beauty text, the more extreme their antagonism becomes. We can say with confidence their negative relationship is never in equilibrium, they too are pure binary opposites who are continually: *out-of-balance.*

If for arguments sake, the *in-balance* associated with Sun and Moon were to be assigned an analogous season, we could call them spring. A time of year when the amount of daylight is exactly equal to the amount of darkness, it is a season *in-balance*. If then we continued with this same method, assigning seasonality to character couplets, then logically autumn would go to the young King and Audience. Again, a season whereby daylight and darkness are *in-balance*. At the other extremes of seasonality, through which both winter and summer are marked as seasons that are *out-of-balance*, we would necessarily assign Cook and Assistant, Talia and Queen, respectfully.

But I believe this not to be analogy, neither is this a mere sophistic trick or rhetorical assignment. These four character couplets and the four seasonal variations just mentioned, are, indeed, metaphorical references. My book, *The Real Sleeping Beauty, Her Meaning & History*, digs deep into this astrological association. And as the evidences are presented, it becomes abundantly clear on why it was Basile choose to name Sleeping Beauty's twin children: Sun and Moon.

Returning now to the brief celestial analysis we mentioned during our binary opposite inquiry, we will begin with the solstices. Two celestial events that although similar, have marked differences in their planetary orientation. One solstice occurs during midwinter when the moon is at its zenith in the night-time sky, a pinnacle that occurs approximately six months after the summer solstice, when its celestial body, the sun, had also reached its highest point during the daylight sky.

They are balanced only by their duration of being equal and opposite through season and by the absence and presence of light. They are seasonal inflections marked through the sun and moon sharing an inverse relationship in which a zenith of one is always at the expense of another, they are then, absolute antagonists.

Contrast those two midseason phenomena with the spring and autumn equinoxes. During these moments their celestial orbs are orientations based on total balance, where the only noticeable difference stems from the leading planetary body, which is interchanged according to season.

For example, after the summer solstice, the moon slowly increases its prominence up until both the celestial bodies are in harmony, the autumn equinox. After the equilibrium has been reached, the moon then starts to gain dominance up until the moment of the lunar solstice (winter zenith) so that the process is then repeated, but now led by the sun, a reversing of the order until a wholly new equilibrium is reached, the spring equinox.

In short, just as the text's binary operations relate to one another: young King vs. Audience, balance; Cook vs. Assistant, antagonism; Sun vs. Moon, balance and Queen vs. Talia, antagonism: annually reoccurring seasons are also bisected, with these same two couplets epitomised through two periods of balance and two periods of antagonism.

If Basile had kept the esoteric pagan script in correlation with changing seasonality, as I argue and shall proceed with the evidence, then we would expect our young King to have had impregnated Talia at approximately the same time of year when the celestial bodies, sun and moon, were phased as *in-balance*. Following the conception scene, the celestial moon would begin to gain dominance, a seasonal period where less light for growth in the plant kingdom becomes manifest, where for all intents and purposes, vegetation is in a state of sleep.

Then, by extension, we should also think Sun and Moon would be born, given their binary relationship, into a period where the celestial bodies are again at a phase of *in-balance*. When light is now at its ascendancy and whereby the celestial sun awakens the plant kingdom; in much the same way, the son awakens Talia by drawing out the spinners flex from the surface of her skin: a metaphor on the first green shoots of spring, breaking the soil's surface.

And indeed, there are a couple of clues explicitly given within Basile's Sleeping Beauty that allows us to start pinpointing and placing together these idealised metaphors, so that those moments of seasonality, marked though celestial periods, balance and antagonism, can be ordered in a correlative way with their binary couplet narratives. The first evidence occurs at the scene just after our young King had stumbled upon the disused palace in which he later finds the sleeping Talia:

> After some considerable time had passed, a young King who enjoyed hunting watched with surprise as his falcon flew into an open palace window. He called out to his hunting

bird. But it failed to return to its perch. Believing the palace to be inhabited, the young King began to knock at its door. He knocked, and knocked. Yet aroused no answer. Impatient, he ordered his attendant to fetch a wine maker's ladder so he could climb into the building; he wanted to know what was inside.

[Sun, Moon and Talia §5]

The first clue for our dating purposes is falconry. In that hunting with falcons has a fairly narrow seasonal window in which the sport takes place. It begins at early autumn and ends during late winter. Another clue, albite only hinted, comes from the mentioning of a wine maker's ladder. Traditionally these are very short stout apparatus who can only be ordinarily used during the grape harvesting period: late August to early September.

Taking then these two clues together, it becomes quite reasonable to assume Talia became impregnated during the autumn period, which further suggests the narration is making a reference to the autumn equinox, an event associated with harmony, a period of being *in-balance.*

With a gestation time lapse approximating nine months, Sun and Moon's birth date would fall within the timeframe of the spring period, again, a moment when their namesake celestial bodies are *in-balance,* which is what we would expect from any astrological features relating to the twin's binary operations.

You shall note that the young King returns to visit Talia during the following autumn when the hunting season has begun again. At this juncture, his twins are approximately six months old; Basile takes this opportunity to write about how our young King continues to use these hunting expeditions as an excuse to make routine calls on his secret love and their two children, a habit that eventually leads to heightening the Queen's suspicion.

Considering some time should have passed between the young King's return and the Queen pressing the Assistant to reveal the young Kings whereabouts, it would not be too unreasonable to suggest all this commotion happens during the winter season: a period in which darkness dominates the domain of man, and at the point in which a celestial antagonism reaches its fullest peak, the lunar solstice, the midwinter season that is *out-of-balance.*

This part of the narrative is marked by reference to the antagonism existing between the Cook vs. Assistant, we also learn that this is the moment when our Cook overcomes the antagonism through refusing to kill the children, and instead of being complicit in an act of barbaric cannibalism, the Cook substitutes Sun and Moon for goat kids.

The final antagonism plays out during the climactic moment of the text and happens between the last binary opposite: Queen vs. Talia. Thus with all thing being equal, from our framework we would expect this antagonism to occur during the last remaining celestial inflection, the summer solstice: again, a seasonal period marked by the twin planetary bodies being in a state of disequilibrium, a season which is *out-of-balance.*

Now this is where our subtext becomes most interesting. When we cross reference these binary operation with the mythemes, then incorporate them into the constellations, we arrive with the final derivatives:

M#1 Conceived: *in-balance* under the constellation of Libra (simulacrum, the Scales)

M#2 Born: *in-balance* under the constellation of Gemini (simulacrum, the Twins)

M#3 Cannibalism: *out-of-balance* but substituted with goat kids under the constellation of Capricornus (simulacrum, the Goat)

M#4 The Queen's downfall: *out-of-balance* under the constellation of Leo (simulacrum, the Lion – see *The Real Sleeping Beauty, Her Meaning & History,* where I argue Talia is none other than the Sumerian Harvest goddess, Inanna, whose totem is a lion).

Before I end this introduction I shall briefly discuss a perfectly valid objection to these star sign allocations, that they do not fit exactly hand in glove with contemporary time conventions, and this is true. However, prior to 750BC annual calendars were not so precise as they are today. This was due in the most part to historic time measures being based on the phases of the moon.

There are also several other reasons why date drift occurred during the early period when the constellations were in their developmental stage, too which I am not going to address right now, but to be sure, the differences between modern and ancient time keeping methods made the latter able and willing to accommodate a myth trying to explain a purposeful personification behind the variations found in the seasons. Whose punctuations, equinox and solstices, were written into the Sleeping Beauty text as inflections points, the mythemes.

This may sound a little obscure, a sticky plaster statement, however, in *The Real Sleeping Beauty, Her Meaning & History* you can read in detail how and why this objection does not hold true. And that from scholarly research, the book also shows evidence that for any text which has aligned the constellations as corresponding to the equinoxes and solstices into one unique concurrent story, must by virtue of the time drift just mentioned, be older than the 750BC.

We end now our preliminary introduction, yet there is one more additional note about this translated Sleeping Beauty text: aspects which were missing from the first edition and subsequently added in later reprints are not presented here. Furthermore, Croce's footnotes and commentaries have also been omitted, this is purely for reasons of clarity.

Sun Moon & Talia

William Le'shon's Sleeping Beauty

From *The Real Sleeping Beauty Her Meaning & History*

(2016)

§1 Long ago, a wise King begot a baby daughter, Talia. He loved her dearly and ordered his great diviners to venture this sweet girl's future. After much confusion, the soothsayers declared Talia would face great dangers from a sliver of flax. Saddened, the old king prohibited linen and hemp thread, spinning wheel and spindle from his palace.

§2 As the years passed, Talia grew into a beautiful young lady. Then one day as she was looking out from her bedroom window, she saw an old lady spinning some thread. Talia had never seen such a sight before. She became curious about the dancing object in the woman's hand, so bid her to bring the spindle and thread to her room; that she may learn more of its mystery.

§3 Inside, Talia took hold of the spindle and began to lay the fibres while the rod danced. But before much time had passed, a sliver of flex entered her finger; under her nail. As though she was dead, she fell to the ground. The old lady ran from the bedroom. Her screams caused a commotion which attracted the courters to Talia's room. When the helpless king stood over his beautiful daughter, he cried a barrel of tears.

§4 In her room, under a brocaded canopy, Talia was placed to rest. The palace, sat at the centre of a large thick forest, had its doors firmly locked. Abandoned forever: the old King could no longer bear the memories of his beautiful daughter.

§5 After some considerable time had passed, a young King who enjoyed hunting watched with surprise as his falcon flew into an open palace window. He called out to his hunting bird. But it failed to return to its perch. Believing the palace to be inhabited, the young King began to knock at its door. He knocked, and knocked. Yet aroused no answer. Impatient, he ordered his attendant to fetch a wine maker's ladder so he could climb into the building; he wanted to know what was inside.

§6 He entered. Then became unsettlingly suspicious, that in every room he search, he found no living person. At last he came across the room where Talia was sat; enchanted. The young King thought she was only sleeping: so called out to her. Quietly at first, but as each call received no answer, he called a little louder.

§7 All along the young King kept admiring her beauty. Soon he turned to lust. Picking her up, he carried the sleeping Talia to her bed, then took the fruits of love. He left her laying on the bed; returning to his own kingdom where he did not remember the sleeping beauty for quite some time.

§8 After many months had passed, Talia gave birth to twins. A boy and girl: two shiny little jewels attended by two fairies who had appeared in the palace. It was them at feeding time who would place the children onto their mother's breasts. One day, when a child wanted some of its mother's milk, the fairies compelled him to grab Talia's finger and suck out the silver flex. The boy coughed, and Talia woke from her deep sleep.

§9 The princess looked down to see her two little beauties by her side. She at once became joyous, squeezing them close to her chest, loving them more than her own life. In her mind though, Talia could not understand what had happened, how it came to be that she was all alone in the palace with her two beautiful babies. Even more mysterious, was how her food magically appeared; not once did she see another living person.

§10 When the hunting season returned, the young King remembered the sleeping beauty. Thinking he could use the hunt to pay her visit.

But to his surprise, he found Talia awake with two miracles of beauty by her side. Shocked, at their wonderfulness, he became unable to move. Then his mouth opened for his confession: that a year earlier, he was enchanted, that he is the children's father.

§11 Quickly they became friends. After several days, soul mates. No sooner than they had fallen in love, the young King took his leave; though not before promising to have Talia brought to his kingdom. Where, on his return, being so enchanted by his experience, that on every hour the young King would chant out the names of Talia, and their two children. Even when he was eating. From his mouth: 'Sun, Moon, Talia'. Neither could sleep abate the young King from saying: 'Sun, Moon, Talia'.

§12 The wife of the young King became suspicious. He was always hunting, and, the chanting: 'Sun, Moon, Talia'. In her chest envy stoked a fire. She summoned the young King's assistant: 'You listen to me,' she said, 'you're between a cliff and an island. Like the jam of the door. Tell me who my husband is in love with, then I shall reward you with riches. But, if you hide from me the truth, then you will not be found either dead, or alive!'

§13 The assistant was fearful, yet felt compelled by greed and self-interest--a badge of honour in the eyes of deprived justice. He decided to lunch on the meat of this faith, replying: 'bread, bread, wine, wine'. Having her suspicion confirmed, she plotted, ordering the assistant to visit Talia. Carrying a false message that the young King was eager to home their children.

§14 Moved by joy, Talia packed their belongings. Then the cold-hearted Medea soon had them in her hands; ordering the Cook to butcher and make different dishes and sauces from the two sweet babies. She demanded he offer them up as food to their wretched father.

§15 The warm-hearted Cook felt only compassion when he saw the two beautiful golden apples. Secretly telling his wife to hide them whilst he set preparing two goat kids in their stead: cooking the goats in a hundred different ways. When at last the hour for dinner had arrived, the Queen personally waited on her husband. Thoroughly enjoying his food, he exclaimed: 'This is good. Oh sweet Mary! By my father's forefathers, I've never had a tastier dish!'.

§16 'Eat, eat. Eat your own'. The Queen encouraged. He paid no attention at first. Too busy devouring the food. Though slowly he became tired of her repeated chants to "eat". He shouted: 'I know well what I eat is mine! You've never brought anything to this house'! Standing in anger, he left for his villa.

§17 Not satisfied by what she believed she had done; the Queen sent again the assistant. He Invited Talia to live under the king's roof, that the young King was impatient for the light of his soul to be near his side. Talia accepted. Unknowing, only the light from a fire awaited her presence.

§18 Soon the princess was brought before the tyrant Queen, whose temperance boasted power and displayed nothing but arrogance, she spoke: 'Welcome, madam dog! So you're the other end of the fabric; the young darling whose enjoying my husband? The evil dog whose made my head twisted and turned! It's right you should come to purgatory, where I will dispense the same pain you've brought onto me!'

§19 Talia apologised, stressing the fault was not hers. It had been the Queen's husband who had taken possession of her body while she slept. The Queen wanted nothing of it. With simple gestures a great fire was lit in the courtyard, readied for Talia. The poor girl seeing herself lost, knelt down. She begged the Queen to give her at least as much time to undress the clothes from her back. 'Undress your clothing'. The Queen consented. Not for mercy, but only to save those robes embroidered with gold and pearls.

§20 She began undressing. Then each time when a piece of clothing was removed, Talia cry out; loudly! With impatience-and already possessing the skirt and coat--the Queen commanded Talia be dragged off to the fire. That from her ashes, soap was to be made for clothes washing. Talia cried-out her last shriek.

§21 Then the Queen noticed the young King's return. He instantly saw Talia and wanted to know what's been happening during his absence. Demanding the whereabouts of his children. To this request the Queen was overjoyed. Revealing the costs of his betrayal. She savored each detail of her revenge: how she'd tricked him into eating his own: Sun and Moon.

§22 Feeling the despair of death, he lamented: 'Am I the werewolf of my own sheep, why did not my veins recognise the same fountain of blood? Ah, barbarian I am. A savage to my kin'. Facing the Queen: 'Go and reap your harvest. Do not send this cruel woman to the courthouse, there shall be no absolution for her.'

§23 His order given and enacted. the Queen along with his Assistant, a handle weaver in this evil game, were both thrown onto the fire. The young King looked towards the Cook; the man he believed to have chopped with knives his children. He Opened his mouth to dictate execution, when the Cook fell to his feet and said: 'actually sir, if I had behaved like those dead persons who were in your service, then I would expect to enter the limekiln of coals, indeed, there is little cost to have a pole behind my back, and I'm sure you would enjoy the entertainment of seeing me twist with numbness as the fire engulfed my body; an honourable harvest for you to see my ashes mixed with those of the Queen.

§24 'But, is this the real thanks I should receive for having saved the children? Despite what that bitter dog wanted: demanding I kill them and return their bodies to the vessel from which they came'.

§25 Hearing these words the young King became overjoyed. He felt as though he was dreaming. He could not believe what had been said. He paused: 'If this statement be true, that you have saved my children from an obscene death. Then I proclaim you will be taken from the turn skewer and placed in the kitchen of my treasure chest to turn. This shall be your reward for making me the happiest man in the world'.

§26 As the young King was saying these words, the Cook's wife, seeing her husband's need, brought out to her king, Sun and Moon. With tears of joy the young King kissed and cuddled Talia and their children; and each one to one another. The Cook was made a gentleman, becoming the young King's assistant. Not long after the young King and Talia were married; a new queen, who enjoyed a lasting life with her husband.

SOLE, LUNA E TALIA

Benedetto Croce's Sleeping Beauty

Modern Italian edition (1932)

Talia, morta per una lisca di lino, è collocata in un palazzo, dove conun re, che vi capita, genera due figli. Vengono essi tutti nelle mani della regina gelosa, che comanda che i figli sieno cotti e dati da mangiare al padre e Talia bruciata. Ma il cuoco salva i figli e Talia è liberata dal re, che fa gettare la moglie nel fuoco apparecchiato per quella.

Il caso delle orche avrebbe potuto indurre qualche brivido di compassione; ma fu causa invece di compiacimento, rallegrandosi tutti che le cose di Parmetella fossero riuscite meglio di come si pensavano. Toccava ora a Popa di ragionare, ed

essa, che stava già coi piedi alla staffa, cosi disse:

È cosa sperimentata che, per lo più, la crudeltà serve da boia a colui stesso che l'esercita, né s'è visto mai che chi sputa in Cielo non gli torni in faccia. E il rovescio di questa medaglia, l'innocenza, è uno scudo di fico, sul quale si spezza o lascia la punta ogni spada di malignità, per modo che, quando un pover'uomo si crede morto e seppellito, allora si vede risuscitare in carne e ossa: come udirete nel racconto

che dalla botte della memoria, col succhiello di questa lingua,

sto per spillare.

C'era una volta un gran signore, il quale, essendogli nata una figlia, a cui die nome Talia, fece venire tutti i sapienti e gl'indovini del suo regno perché le dicessero la ventura.

Costoro, dopo vari consulti, conclusero che essa era esposta a gran pericolo a causa di una lisca di lino. E il re proibì che in casa sua entrasse mai lino o canapa o altra roba simile, per evitare ogni cattivo incontro.

Ora, essendo Talia grandicella e stando alla finestra, vide passare una vecchia che filava; e, poiché non aveva mai visto né conocchia né fuso, piacendole assai quel danzare che il fuso faceva, fu presa da curiosità e la fece venir su, e, tolta in mano la rocca, cominciò a stendere il filo. Ma, per disgrazia, una lisca le entrò nell'unghia e subito cadde a terra morta. La vecchia, a tanta disavventura, scappò che ancora salta a precipizio per le scale; e lo sventurato padre, dopo aver pagato con un barile di lacrime una secchia di asprinio, collocò la morta Talia in quello stesso palazzo, che era in un bosco, seduta su una sedia di velluto, sotto un baldacchino di broccato. Poi, serrate le porte, abbandonò per sempre la casa, cagione di tanto suo male, per cancellare in tutto e per tutto dalla memoria la sciagura sofferta.

Dopo qualche tempo, a un re, che andava a caccia per quei luoghi, sfuggì un falcone e volò a una finestra di quella casa; né tornando al richiamo, il re fece picchiare alla porta, credendo che la casa fosse abitata. Ma, dopo aver bussato invano lunga pezza, il re, domandala una scala da vendemmiatore, volle di persona scalare la casa e vedere che cosa ci fosse dentro. Salito ed entrato, rimase stupito, non trovando in nessun luogo persona vivente; e, in ultimo, giunse alla camera, dove stava Talia come incantata.

Il re, credendo che dormisse, la chiamò. Ma, non ritornando quella in sé, per quanto facesse e gridasse, e, intanto, essendosi egli acceso di quelle bellezze, la portò di peso sopra un letto e ne colse i frutti d'amore, e, lasciandola coricata, se ne tornò al suo regno, dove non si ricordò più per lungo tempo di quel caso.

Dopo nove mesi, Talia partorì una coppia di bambini, un maschio e una femmina, due monili splendenti, che, governati da due fate, apparse in quel palazzo, furono da esse posti alle mammelle della madre. E una volta che i bambini, volendo succhiare, non riuscivano a trovare il capezzolo, si misero in bocca proprio quel dito che era stato punto, e tanto lo succhiarono che ne trassero fuori la lisca. Subito parve che Talia si svegliasse da un gran sonno; e, vedutesi quelle due gioie accanto, porse loro il petto e le tenne care quanto la vita. Ma non sapeva rendersi conto di quel che le era accaduto, trovandosi sola sola in quel palazzo e con due figli allato, e vedendosi portare quel che le occorreva per mangiare senza scorgere persona alcuna.

Il re, un giorno, si ricordò dell'avventura con la bella dormente, e, presa occasione da una nuova caccia in quei luoghi, venne a vederla. E, avendola ritrovata desta e con quei due prodigi di bellezza, ne ebbe un piacere da stordire. A Talia raccontò allora chi egli era e come era andato il fatto; e fecero tra loro amicizia e lega grande, ed egli rimase parecchi giorni in sua compagnia. Poi si accommiatò con promessa

di venirla a prendere e condurla al suo regno; e, intanto, tornato a casa sua, nominava a ogni ora Talia e i figli. Se mangiava, aveva Talia sulla bocca, e Sole e Luna (che questi erano i nomi dei bambini); se si coricava, chiamava l'una e gli altri.

La moglie del re, che già dall'indugiare il marito a caccia aveva avuto qualche lampo di sospetto, a queste invocazioni di Talia, Luna e Sole fu presa da altro calore che di sole; e perciò, chiamato il segretario, gli disse: 'Ascolta, figlio mio: tu stai tra Scilla e Cariddi, tra lo stipite e la porta, tra la grata e la sbarra. Se tu mi dici di chi mio marito è innamorato, ti fo ricco; e, se mi nascondi la verità, non ti fo più trovare né morto né vivo'. E colui, da una parte sconvolto dalla paura, dall'altra tirato dall'interesse, che è una fascia agli occhi dell'onore, una benda della giustizia, uno sferracavallo della fede, le disse pane pane e vino vino.

Allora la regina mandò lo stesso segretario in nome del re a Talia, facendole dire che egli voleva rivedere i figli; ed essa, con grande gioia, glieli inviò. Ma quel cuore di Medea, tosto che li ebbe tra le mani, ordinò al cuoco di scannarli e farne diversi manicaretti e salse per darli a mangiare al misero padre.

Il cuoco, che era tenerino di polmone, al vedere quei due aurei pomi di bellezza, ne sentì pietà, e, affidatili alla moglie perché li nascondesse, apparecchiò due capretti in cento varie pietanze. Quando fu l'ora del desinare, la regina fece portare le vivande; e, mentre il re mangiava di gran gusto, esclamando:

'Com'è buono questo, per la vita di Lanfusa!', o 'Com'è saporito quest'altro, per l'anima di mio nonno!',

Essa lo incoraggiava, dicendogli:

'Mangia, che mangi del tuo'.

Il re, per due o tre volte, non fece attenzione a queste pnrole; ma poi, udendo la musica che continuava, rispose:

'So bene che mangio del mio, perché tu non hai portato niente

in questa casa'.

E, levatosi con collera, se ne andò a una villa poco lontana per acquietarsi.

Non ancora sazia la regina di quanto credeva di aver fatto, mandò di nuovo il segretario a chiamare la stessa Talia, col pretesto che il re l'aspettava; ed essa venne immediatamente, desiderosa di trovare la sua luce e non sapendo che l'attendeva il fuoco. Condotta innanzi alla regina, costei, con un volto da Nerone, tutta inciprignita, le disse:

'Sii la benvenuta, madama Troccola! Tu sei quella fine stoffa, quella buon'erba

che ti godi mio marito? Tu sei quella cagna malvagia, che mi fa stare con tante giravolte di capo? Va', che sei giunta al purgatorio, dove ti farò scontare il danno che mi hai fatto!'

Talia cominciò a scusarsi che la colpa non era sua e che il marito aveva preso possessione dei suoi territori mentre essa era adoppiata. Ma la regina non volle intendere scuse, e, fatto accendere in mezzo allo stesso cortile del palazzo un

gran fuoco, comandò che ve la gettassero dentro.

La misera, che si vide perduta, inginocchiatasi dinanzi a lei, la supplicò che le desse almeno tanto tempo da spogliarsi dei vestiti che aveva addosso. E la regina, non tanto per Misericordia verso la sventurata quanto per risparmiare quegli abiti ricamati d'oro e di perle, le disse:

'Spogliati, che mi contento.'

Cominciò Talia a spogliarsi, e a ogni pezzo di vestito clie si toglieva dalla persona gettava uno strido; tanto che, essendosi già tolta la roba, la gonna e il giubbone, quando fu a togliersi il sottanino, gettò l'ultimo strido, mentre al tempo stesso la trascinavano a fare la cenerata per l'acqua bollente da lavare le brache a Caronte. Ma, in quel punto, accorse il re, che, visto lo spettacolo, volle sapere tutto l'accaduto. E, avendo domandato dei figli, udi dalla stessa moglie, che gli rinfacciava il tradimento usatole, come glieli avesse fatti mangiare.

Il re si die in preda alla disperazione:

'Dunque, sono stato io stesso -- gridava -- lupomannaro delle mie pecorelle?

Oimè, e perché le vene mie non conobbero la fontana del loro stesso sangue? Ah, turca rinnegata, e quale ferocia è stata la tua? Va', che tu raccoglierai i torsoli, e non manderò cotesta faccia di tiranno al Colosseo per la penitenza!'

Cosi dicendo, ordinò che la regina fosse gettata nello stesso fuoco acceso per Talia, e insieme con essa il segretario, che era stato maniglia di questo tristo giuoco e tessitore della malvagia trama; e voleva fare il medesimo del cuoco, che credeva avesse tritato con la coltella i figli suoi. Ma questi gli si gettò ai piedi e gli disse:

'Veramente, signore, non ci vorrebbe altra piazza morta pel servigio che ti ho reso che una calcara di bragia; non ci vorrebbe altro aiuto di costa che un palo dietro; non ci vorrebbe altro trattenimento che di storcermi e rattrappirmi nel fuoco; non ci vorrebbe altro onore che di veder mischiate le ceneri di un cuoco con quelle di una regina! Ma non è questo il ringraziamento che attendo per averti salvato i figli, a dispetto di quel fiele di cane, che voleva farli uccidere per restituire al corpo tuo quello che era parte dello stesso corpo.'

Il re, che udi queste parole, restò fuori di sé e gli pareva di sognare, né poteva credere quello che le sue orecchie sentivano. Poi, rivolto al cuoco, disse:

'Se è vero che mi hai salvato i figli, sta' pur sicuro che ti toglierò dal girare gli spiedi e ti porrò nella cucina di questo petto a girare, come a te piacerà, le voglie mie, dandoti premi tali che ti chiamerai felice al mondo.'

Mentre il re diceva queste parole, la moglie del cuoco, che vide il bisogno del marito, portò Luna e Sole dinanzi al padre, il quale, giocando a tre con la moglie e i figli, faceva mulinello di baci or con l'uno or con l'altro. E, data grossa mancia al cuoco e fattolo gentiluomo suo di camera, si prese in moglie Talia, la quale godette lunga vita col marito e i figli, conoscendo a tutta prova che.

Quei ch'ha ventura, il bene

anche dormendo, ottiene.

SOLE, LUNA E TALIA

Giovan Battista Basile's Sleeping Beauty

'Lo Cunto de li Cunti' (1634)

Talia, morta pe na resta de lino, è lassata a no palazzo, dove capitato no re 'nce fa dui figlie. La mogliere gelosa l'ha ne le mano e commanda che li figlie siano date a magnare cuotte a lo patre e Talia sia abbrusciata: lo cuoco salva li figlie e Talia è liberata da lo re, facenno iettare la mogliera a lo stisso fuoco apparecchiato pe Talia.

Dove lo caso dell'orche poteva portare quarche frecola de compassione addusse causa de gusto, rallegrannose ognuno che le cose de Parmetella fossero resciute assai meglio de chello che se penzava. Dopo lo quale cunto toccanno a Popa de ragioniare essa, che steva co li piede a la staffa, cossì decette:

Era na vota no gran signore, ch'essendole nata na figlia

chiammata Talia fece venire li sacciente e 'nevine de lo regno suio a direle la ventura. Li quale, dapo' varie consiglie, concrusero ca passava gran pericolo pe na resta de lino: pe la quale cosa fece na proibizione che dintro la casa soia non ce trasesse né lino né cannavo o autra cosa semele, pe sfoire sto male scuntro.

Ma, essenno Talia grannecella e stanno a la fenestra, vedde passare na vecchia che filava; e, perché n'aveva visto mai conocchia né fuso e piacennole assai chello ro-cioliare che faceva, le venne tanta curiositate che la fece saglire 'ncoppa, e, pigliato la rocca 'mano, commenzaie a stennere lo filo, ma pe desgrazia, trasutole na resta de lino dintro l'ogna, cadette morta 'n terra.

La quale cosa visto la vecchia ancora zompa pe le scale a bascio. E lo nigro patre, 'ntiso la desgrazia soccessa, dapo' avere pagate co varrile de lagreme sto cato d'asprinio, la pose, dintro a lo medesimo palazzo che steva 'n campagna, seduta a na seggia de velluto, sotta a no bardacchino de 'mbroccato, e, chiuso le porte, abbannonaie pe sempre chillo palazzo, causa de tanto danno suio, pe scordarese 'n tutto e pe tutto la memoria de sta desgrazia.

Ma ienno fra certo tiempo no re a caccia e, scappato-le, no farcone volaie dintro na fenestra de chella casa né tornanno a rechiammo, fece tozzolare la porta, credenno che 'nce abbitasse gente. Ma, dapo' tozzolato no buono piezzo, lo re, fatto venire na scala de vennegnato-re, voze de perzona scaliare sta casa e vedere che cosa nce fosse dintro e, sagliuto 'ncoppa e trasuto pe tutto, restaie na mummia non trovannoce perzona vivente.

All'utemo arrivaie a la cammara dove steva Talia comme 'ncantata, che vista da lo re, credennose che dormesse, la chiammaie; ma, non revenenno pe quanto facesse e gridasse e pigliato de caudo de chelle bellezze, portatola de pesole a no lietto ne couze li frutte d'ammore e, lassatola corcata, se ne tornaie a lo regno suio, dove non se allecordaie pe no piezzo de chesto che l'era socciesso.

La quale, dapo' nove mise, scarricaie na cocchia de criature, uno mascolo e l'autra femmena, che vedive dui vranchiglie de gioie, li quale covernate da doi fate che comparzero a chillo palazzo, le posero a le zizze de la mamma. Li quale, na vota, volenno zucare né trovanno lo capetiello, l'afferraro lo dito e tanto zucaro che ne tiraro l'aresta, pe la quale cosa parze che se scetasse da no gran suonno e, vistose chelle gioie a canto, le dette zizza e le tenne care quanto la vita.

E mentre non sapeva che l'era accascato trovannose sola sola dintro a chillo palazzo, e co dui figlie a lato, e vedennose portare quarche refrisco de magnare senza vedere la perzona, lo re, allecordato de Talia, pigliato accasione de ire a caccia venne a vederela e, trovatola scetata e co dui cucchepinte de bellezza, appe no gusto da stordire. E, ditto a Talia chi era e comm'era passato lo fatto, fecero n'amecizia e na lega granne e se stette na mano de iuorne cod essa, e, lecenziatose co prommessa de tornare e portarenella, iette a lo regno suio, nome-nanno a tutt'ore Talia e li figlie, tale che se manciava aveva Talia 'mocca e Sole e Luna, che cossì dette nomme a li figlie, si se corcava chiammava l'uno e l'autro.

La mogliere de lo re, che de la tardanza a la caccia de lo marito aveva pigliato quarche sospetto, co sso chiammare de Talia, Luna e Sole l'era pigliato autro caudo che de sole e perzò, chiammatose lo secretario le decette:
 'Siente cca, figlio mio: tu stai fra Sciglia e Scariglia, fra lo stantaro e la porta, tra la mazza agghionta e la grata. Si tu me dici di chi sta 'nammorato maritemo io te faccio ricco e si tu me nascunne sto fatto io non te faccio trovare né muorto né vivo.'

Lo compare, da na parte scommuoppeto de la paura, dall'autra scannato da lo 'nteresse, ch'è na pezza all'uocchie de l'onore, n'appannatora de la iostizia, na sferraca-vallo de la fede, le disse de lo pane pane e de lo vino vi-no, pe la quale cosa la regina mannaie lo stisso secretario 'nome de lo re a Talia, ca voleva vedere li figlie. La quale co n'allegrezza granne mannatole, chillo core de Medea commannaie a lo cuoco che l'avesse scannate e fattone deverse menestrelle e saporielle, pe farele magnare a lo nigro marito.

Lo cuoco, ch'era teneriello de permone, visto sti dui belle pumme d'oro n'avette compassione e, datole a la mogliere soia che li nasconnesse, apparecchiaie dui crapette 'n cento fogge.

E venuto lo re, la regina co no gusto granne fece venire le vivanne e, mentre lo re mangiava co no gusto granne dicenno:
 'Oh comme è buono chesto, pre vita de Lanfusa! oh comm'è bravo chest'autro, pe l'arma de vavomo!'
 Essa sempre deceva:
 'Magna, ca de lo tuo man-ge!'
 Lo re doi o tre vote non mese arecchie a sto taluorno, all'utemo, sentuto ca continuava la museca, respose:
 'Saccio ca magno lo mio, perché non ce hai portato niente a sta casa!

e, auzatose co collera, se ne iette a na villa poco lontano a sfocare la collera.'

Ma fra sto miezo, non sazia la regina de quanto aveva fatto, chiammato de nuovo lo secretario mannaie a chiammare Talia co scusa ca lo re l'aspettava, la quale a la stessa pedata se ne venne desiderosa de trovare la luce soia, non sapenno ca l'aspettava lo fuoco. Ma, arrivata

'nanze la regina, essa, co na facce de Nerone tutta 'nvi-perata, le disse: 'Singhe la benvenuta, madamma Troccola! tu sì chella fina pezza, chella mal'erva che te gaude maritemo? tu sì chella cana perra che me fave stare co tanta sbotamiente de chiocca? và ca sì benuta a lo pur-gaturo, dove te scontarraggio lo danno che m'haie fatto!'

Talia, sentenno chesto, commenzaie a scusarese ca non era corpa soia e ca lo marito aveva pigliato possessione de lo terretorio suio quanno essa era addobbiata. Ma la regina, non volenno 'ntennere scuse, fece allommare dintro a lo stisso cortiglio de lo palazzo no gran

focarone e commannaie che 'nce l'avessero schiaffata 'miezo. Talia, che vedde le cose male arrivate, 'ngenocchiatase 'nante ad essa la pregaie c'a lo manco le desse tanto tiempo che se spogliasse li vestite c'aveva 'n cuollo. La regina, non tanto pe meserecordia de la negra giovane quanto pe avanzare chille abete racamate d'oro e de perne, disse:
 'Spogliate, ca me contento.'

E Talia commenzata a spogliarese, ogne piezzo de vestito che se levava iettava no strillo: tanto che, avennose levato la robba, la gonnella e lo ieppone, comme fu a lo levarese de lo sottaniello, iettato l'utemo strillo, tanno la strascinavano a fare cennerale pe lo scaudatiello de le brache de Caronte, quanno corze lo re e, trovato sto spettacolo, voze sapere tutto lo fatto, e, demannato de li figlie, sentette da la stessa mogliere, che le renfacciava lo tredemiento recevuto, comme 'nce l'aveva fatto cannariare.

La quale cosa sentuto lo nigro re, datose 'm preda de la desperazione, commenzaie a dicere:

'Adonca so' stato io medesemo lupo menaro de le pecorelle meie! ohimè, e pecché le vene meie non canoscettero le fontane de lo stisso sango? ah, torca renegata e che canetude-ne cosa è stata la toia? và ca tu ne iarraie pe le torza e non mannarraggio ssa facce de tiranno a lo Culiseo pe penetenzia!'

E, cossì decenno, ordenaie che fosse iettata a lo stisso fuoco allommato pe Talia e 'nziemme cod essa lo secretario che fu maniglia de sto ammaro iuoco e tessetore de sta marvasa tramma; e, volenno fare lo medesemo de lo cuoco che se pensava c'avesse adacciariato li figli, isso iettatose a li piede de lo re le disse:

'Veramente, segnore, non ce vorria autra chiazza morta pe lo servizio che t'aggio fatto che na carcara de vrase, non ce vorria autro aiuto de costa che no palo dereto, non 'nce vorria autro trattenimiento che stennerire e arronchiare dintro a lo fuoco, non 'nce vorria autro vantaggio ch'essere mescate le cennere de no cuoco co chelle de na regina! ma non è chesta la gran merzè che aspetto d'averete sarvato le figlie a despietto de chillo fele de cane, che le voleva accidere pe tornare a lo cuorpo tuio chello ch'era parte de lo stisso cuorpo.'

Lo re, che sentette ste parole, restaie fora de se stisso e le pareva de 'nzonnarese, né poteva credere chello che sentevano l'aurecchie soie; po', votatose a lo cuoco, le disse:
 'Si è lo vero che m'haie sarvate li figlie singhe pu-ro securo ca te levarraggio da votare li spite e te mettarraggio a la cocina de sto pietto a votare comme te piace le voglie meie, dannote premmio tale che te chiammarraie felice a lo munno!'

Fra tanto che lo re deceva ste parole, la mogliere de lo cuoco, che vedde lo besuogno de lo marito, portai la Luna e lo Sole 'nanze lo patre, lo quale iocanno a lo tre co la mogliere e li figlie faceva moleniello de vase mo coll'uno e mo coll'autro; e, dato no gruosso veveraggio a lo cuoco e fattolo gentelommo de la cammara soia, se pigliaie Talia pe mogliere, la quale gaudette longa vita co lo marito e co li figlie,

canoscenno a tutte botte ca a chi
ventura tene

Quanno dorme perzì chiove lo bene.

Printed in Great Britain
by Amazon